The Locked Room

KT-591-978

Contents

1

A Meeting

A big man in a suit walked into a bar.
It was a small, quiet bar
in a country pub.
Sitting by the fire in the corner
was a thin old man.
He looked up when the big man came in.
'You must be Harry Crabbe,' he said.

'That's me,' said the big man,
in a loud, booming voice.
'Harry Crabbe, ghost-hunter.'
He shook the old man's hand.
His grip was so tight the old man
gasped in pain.
'And you must be Sam Jaffet.
What are you drinking?'

'Whisky,' said the old man.

Harry bought two whiskies.
He sat down next to the old man.
'Right,' he said.
'Let's get down to business.
You answered my advert.
You say your house is haunted.'

'I don't just say it,' said the old man. 'It is.'

Harry laughed loudly.
'Well, we'll see.
Thing is, I'm interested in haunted houses.
So-called haunted houses.
It's my job. I write about them.'

'Really,' said the old man.
He didn't seem very interested.
He drank some whisky.
He coughed.

'Yes,' said Harry.
'And I'd like to spend the night in your house.'

'No, you wouldn't,' said the old man.

'I would,' said Harry.
'Take me there tonight.
I'll pay you.
I'll pay you well.'

'I wouldn't spend the night in that house
for a million pounds,' said the old man.

'What – you don't live there?'

'Not any more.'
The old man shivered.
'I've got a room here, in the inn.
I wouldn't live in that house again
even if you paid me to.'

'So the house is empty?'
said Harry.

'No, it's not empty,' said the old man.
'It's full of ghosts.'

2

The House on the Hill

'Full of ghosts, eh?' said Harry Crabbe.
'Listen – I know about ghosts.
I've slept in haunted houses.
Hundreds of them.
So-called haunted houses.
All over the country.
I've written books about them.
I've never seen a ghost yet.'

'You ain't never stayed in my house,'
said the old man.

'Where is it?
Is it near here?'

'I'll show you, if you like.'
The old man got stiffly to his feet.
Harry followed him to the door of the pub.

The old man pointed along the dark road.
On top of a hill,
Harry saw an old, creepy-looking house.
It was lit up in the moonlight.
A lonely house, standing by itself.
A couple of miles away, Harry thought.

'That's it?'

'That's it,' said the old man.
He went back to his seat.
Harry followed.
'I was left that house in my father's will,'
said the old man.

'Mind, he never lived there.
Nobody's lived there for years.
But I tried.
Oh yes, I tried.'
He shivered again.
'One night was enough for me.'

'Well, let me try, too,' said Harry.

The old man shook his head.
'You wouldn't come out alive.'

Harry was getting a bit angry.
'Why did you answer my advert, then?'

'Thought you just wanted to talk about it.'

'Well, talk about it, then!'

'All right,' said the old man.
'I don't mind doing that.'

3

Ghosts

'Have another drink,' said Harry.

'Thanks,' said the old man.
He sipped his whisky.
'That house is haunted by –
oh, I don't know how many ghosts.
A man hanged himself there.
His ghost haunts the landing.
Then there was a nun.
She was walled up there.
Her ghost haunts the cellar.

Then there was another man.
He got his head cut off.
His ghost haunts the garden.'

'Right,' said Harry.
He wanted to laugh.
He had heard stuff like this
so many times before.
'Did you see any of these ghosts?'

The old man drank some more whisky.
He coughed.
'Not see, exactly.
Not see with my eyes.
But I heard noises.
And I felt them.
I knew they were there.
A strong feeling of evil, there was.'

'Really?' said Harry.

'Yes, really,' said the old man sharply.
'The worst feeling came from –
the locked room.'

'The locked room?'

'Yes, the room at the end of the hall.
Locked door.
They say a man was locked up in there.
Back in the olden days.
Left to starve.
They say his skeleton's still in there.
He was chained to the wall.'

'Why didn't you open it and find out?'

'Didn't have the key,' said the old man.
'But I wouldn't have opened it anyway.
There was evil in that room.
You could feel it.'

'Yeah, right,' said Harry.
What a load of rubbish, he was thinking.
His trip here had been a waste of time.
Unless he could get to stay the night
in the house.
That would give him something
to write about.

'Listen, Mr Jaffet,' he said. 'Why not let me
stay there on my own?
I'll pay you.
Look, here's a hundred pounds.'
He threw the money on the table.
'What do you say?'

4

Harry Drives Away

The old man pushed the money away.
'I don't want your money.
And I don't want you going up to the house.
You wouldn't come out alive.
Take my advice.
Just drive away.
Go home to your safe, warm bed.'

Harry wanted to tell the old man
that he wasn't afraid.
Harry didn't believe in ghosts.
He'd slept in hundreds of 'haunted houses'.
He was none the worse for it.
But what was the point, Harry thought.
The old man was as stubborn as a mule.

'All right,' he said.
'But tell me this –
if you can't live in the house,
why don't you sell it?'

The old man laughed a thin, dry laugh.
'No one would buy it.
No one round here goes anywhere near
that house.
They all know it's haunted.
Ain't that right, Joe?'

'That's right, Sam,' said the barman.

'All right,' said Harry.
It was no good.
The old man would not change his mind.
He finished his drink and stood up.
'Thanks for talking to me.'

'That's all right,' said Sam Jaffet.
'Now you just drive home
to your safe, warm bed.'

'I will,' said Harry.

But he didn't.

5

An Open Door

Harry got into his car.
He drove up the hill
towards the haunted house.
The road was narrow and twisty.
It was further than it looked.
More like four miles.
He didn't pass a single house
or car on the way.

At the top he looked back
down the hill.
He could see the little lights of the
village below.
If he had to call for help from up here,
no one would ever hear him.

Don't be silly, he told himself.
He'd be OK.
He drove through the gates of the house.
He went up a long drive.

The house loomed up before him.
It looked old and creepy.
Like the house of the Addams family.

He got out of the car.
He slammed the door.
It sounded very loud in the quiet of the night.

He walked up to the house.
He went through the garden.
The man with no head
was meant to haunt this bit.
But Harry couldn't see him.

His footsteps crunched on the path.
The moon had gone behind a cloud now.
It was very dark.
Harry had a torch in his pocket.
He shone it at the front of the house.
He was looking for an open window.
If there wasn't one he'd break in, of course.

But then he saw that the front door was open.
It was wide open.
It was as if the house was waiting for him.

Harry didn't think twice.
He shone the torch in front of him.
He went up the steps and into the dark house.

6

The Locked Room

The hall was dark and dusty.
Harry shone his torch around the walls.
The paint was peeling.
Old pictures hung on the walls.

A sudden noise made him jump.
He saw a rat run across the hall.
Harry smiled.
No ghosts here.
Just rats.

He shone his torch into the rooms
on each side of the hall.
There was some old furniture.
It was damp and mildewed.
Nothing of interest.

The floorboards creaked
as he walked down the hall.
There, at the end, was the locked room.

Harry tried the handle.
It wouldn't budge.
There was no key, just as the old man
had said.

Harry badly wanted to get in there.
If there was a skeleton, he'd have a story.
You'd get good money
for a story like that.

He tried kicking the door.
He tried barging his shoulder against it.
But it wouldn't budge.
It was solid oak.
He'd never break it down.

Harry gave it up.

He went off to look round the rest of the house.

Shining his torch in front of him, Harry went up the stairs.

7

The Key

Harry stood on the landing.
He looked around him.
It was meant to be haunted
by the ghost of the hanged man.
But he saw nothing, of course.
Just a few rats running
from the beam of Harry's torch.

He shone the torch into all the rooms.
There was an old grandfather clock.
An old rocking horse.
No ghosts, of course.
Harry didn't expect any.
He loved stories about ghosts,
but he didn't believe in them.

He made his way downstairs.
He'd just check the cellar.
He wanted to find the ghost of the nun.
Then he would find a room to bed down in.
It was important to stay the night.
Then he could say
he'd really checked the place out.

As he went through the hall,
he shone his torch
on the door of the locked room again.
It was a pity he couldn't get in . . .

Then a thrill went through him.
The key was in the lock.
He could have sworn it wasn't there before.
But it was there now.

8

Shut In!

Harry turned the key of the locked room.
He pushed the door open.
He stepped inside and shone
his torch around.

The room was bare.
Stone walls, and a stone floor.
There were iron bars at the window.
You could die in here, he thought.
You'd never get out of here.

The trouble was,
there was no skeleton.
The old man's story wasn't even true.

'Silly old fool,' said Harry out loud.
'There's no skeleton here.'

'Not yet,' said a thin, high voice.
'But there will be.'

The big oak door swung shut
behind Harry.
He heard the key turn in the lock.
Then a small, high-pitched laugh.
Then silence.
Harry beat on the door for a long, long time.
But nobody came to open it.
Not that night,
or any other night.